Creating Delight

Connecting Gratitude, Humor, and Play for all Ages

Kathy Laurenhue
with Bron Roberts
and Sharon Wall

Creating Delight: Connecting Gratitude, Humor, and Play for All Ages
By Kathy Laurenhue, M.A., with Bronwyn Roberts and Sharon Wall

ISBN: 0-9786362-4-4 – Creating Delight - print

© 2016 Kathy Laurenhue

Kathy@WiserNow.com

www.WiserNow.com

All rights reserved

Pure joy jumps from every page of this inspiring book: "Creating Delight: Connecting Gratitude, Humor and Play for all Ages". The vast experience of the authors, Kathy Laurenhue with Bron Roberts and Sharon Wall is evident in the rich content and abundant resources found in this gem. This is that rare kind of book that can be flipped open to any page treating the reader to ideas that are sure to delight. Colorful pictures and creative designs emerge on every single page of this captivating treasure. From crafting gratitude trees to reflections on sharing rituals, this book is a must read for all interested in finding and living life with great joy. This book has my highest recommendation.

—Mary Kay Morrison, author of Using Humor to Maximize Living, educator, consultant, past-president of the Association of Applied and Therapeutic Humor

While Creating Delight certainly does that in a big way with lots of easy-to-create "gratitude trees" and other fun projects, what spoke to me most about this book was the brief chapter on "Giving and Receiving Compliments."

I was struck by the words in this section because it is such a simple idea, and one that many authors miss, when seeking more ways to be grateful.

It is so easy to give a compliment or praise someone. It takes nothing away from you yet provides the receiver with a joyful and uplifting moment. And, although I haven't done any scientific research on this, I bet that the giver of the compliment is enriched too.

For this idea alone, this book is a godsend.

—Allen Klein, author of You Can't Ruin My Day and numerous other books

This book as its name implies, is delightful! Different from "gratitude" and the book is a lovely reminder to look for or create delight in our lives. After reading the book I started my own "delight" journal, making notes about the "delights" in my everyday life. There are so many creative ways to show delight, easy, inexpensive and brings us back from the negative news that seems to be what makes "headlines", our constant check on the cell phone, and how many of us are tied to the computer. Thank you for this wonderful reminder to look for and find joy in the many delights that surround us all.

— Joyce Simard, author of The Namaste Care Program for People with Dementia

Creating Delight is an uplifting and enjoyable read that has universal appeal. The author not only connects gratitude to humor and play but provides techniques for giving and receiving compliments for those who find this social skill sometimes awkward. Chapter 3 focuses on how to visually display gratitude. The colorful photos made me want to run to the nearest craft store and begin a new project . . . I loved the section describing rituals and have added some of the suggestions to my own gratitude practice. The resource pages are invaluable and encourage the reader to continue their gratitude journey.

I found this book to be absolutely deLIGHTful!

—Jill Knox, Healthy Humor Award-winner, peace activist, founder of the Funny Side

This wonderful book is chockful of fun and creative ideas. Just reading it fills me with happiness and creative energies. I especially liked all the photos showing creations. The book is really well done!

—Karen Love, gerontologist, co-founder and Executive Director at Dementia Action Alliance

Table of Contents

CHAPTER 1
Defining and connecting elements of delight —
Why we wrote this book 13

CHAPTER 2
Starting with the basics: Giving and receiving
compliments 23

CHAPTER 3
Visual varieties of creating expressions of delight and
gratitude 29

CHAPTER 4
Alternative creating delight rituals 81

Resources 99

About us 111

Our workshops and products and contact info 113

Opening words

People usually consider walking on water or in thin air a miracle.
But I think the real miracle is not to walk either on water or in thin air,
but to walk on earth.
Every day we are engaged in a miracle which we don't even recognize:
a blue sky, white clouds, green leaves,
the black, curious eyes of a child—our own two eyes.
All is a miracle.

— Thich Nhat Hanh

A person will be called to account on Judgment Day
for every permissible thing he might have enjoyed but did not.

— paraphrased from the Talmud

Happiness never decreases by being shared.

— Buddha

Preface

Among the synonyms for delight are these: great pleasure, happiness, joy, bliss, enchantment, charm, elation, and amusement. We could have used several of those words in our title, and indeed debated doing so, but I (Kathy) advocated for delight because I have always been partial to words that are related to light—daylight, sunlight, moonlight, starlight, twilight, candlelight, highlights, lightheartedness, lightness of being, enlighten. They all seem to bring an uplifting clarity to life. Furthermore, the word delight has an element of unexpected surprise to it—something likely to bring laughter and joy and a sense of being connected to others. If we can be delighted daily and bring delight to others, our lives will be rich indeed.

Therefore, using all these words and synonyms:

The aim of this book is to illustrate concrete ways you can bring that delight to others you serve — students/children, older adults, your family and friends.

A great deal has been written about gratitude and mindfulness in recent years, and we are in absolute agreement with the inspiring authors who tout their importance. At the same time, we have felt a need for 1) broadening the possibilities for gratitude, 2) a more lighthearted attitude toward mindfulness, and 3) specific ideas for sharing the pleasures of being alive—in other words, bringing delight to life.

> *Laughter is carbonated holiness.*
>
> — ANNE LAMOTT
>
> *Laughter is grace in its gaseous form.*
>
> — CATHLEEN FALSANI

All three of us are strong believers in humor as humankind's best coping tool. Bron and I are active in the Association of Applied and Therapeutic Humor (AATH—See Resources) and are both Certified Humor Professionals. Sharon has a long standing association with the Clown Doctors and Humour Foundation through a valued association with the wonderful and much loved Peter Spitzer (1946-2014). All three of us use humor as a teaching and healing tool, and particularly as a means of connecting with others, of finding common ground. My mantra on the Wiser Now website has for years been:

> *Laughter builds rapport.*
>
> *Rapport builds trust.*
>
> *Trust builds relationships.*

Better relationships and greater understanding of one another is the outcome we are aiming for when you read this book.

But whereas that's the aim of many other authors, we are adding an emphasis on cheerfulness and play as a means to that end. We hope you enjoy the exercises and encourage you to let us know if you have ideas to add.

Contact us at info@CreatingDelight.com. Also visit our Facebook page and add your comments at **https://wwww.facebook.com/creatingdelight/**.

Chapter 1

Defining and connecting elements of delight—Why we wrote this book

Since you cannot do good to all, you are to pay special attention to those who, by the accidents of time, or place, or circumstances, are brought into closer connection with you.

— Saint Augustine

If there there is one word in the title of this book that is more important than all the others, it is "connecting." The need for strong social networks — people we value and who value us in return — has been shown by research in recent years to be one of the most important elements for wellbeing at all ages, but particularly in aging. It is narrowly beaten in aging by physical exercise, which is good for both body and brain and helps with our emotional wellbeing, too. Other factors like a healthy diet, being a non-smoker, and being financially stable all have a role, but it is our connection to others that makes life worth living. Therefore, in our view, it is the single most important element of wellbeing.

Our Resources section is filled with authors we admire who make a strong case for gratitude, humor, and play, as well as for the related subjects of mindfulness, meditation, happiness and more. Our goal is not to repeat their arguments, but to connect those elements and help you create delight wherever you may work, study, or live.

This chapter briefly summarizes some of the key points of leaders in these broad fields thereby giving you reasons to try out the many practical applications for connecting to others in the chapters that follow. But what we hope sets us apart from those experts is precisely those applications. We wrote this book to help you see how you can invite your *gratitude* and sense of *humor* out to *play*.

A brief overview of expert opinions

Vivek Murthy, MD, MBA, the current U.S. Surgeon General, is a strong proponent of the idea that happiness is open to all. In a TEDMED talk (**http://www.tedmed.com/talks/show?id=527633**) he noted, "Happiness affects us on a biological level. Happy people have lower levels of cortisol, a key stress hormone." In addition, he noted, that happy people "have more favorable heart rates and blood pressure levels. They have strong immune systems . . . and lower levels of inflammatory markers . . . linked to coronary heart disease. It turns out that even when you control for smoking, physical activity, and other health behaviors, happy people live longer. There's something about happiness that seems to be protective."

He identified four tools for increasing happiness — meditation, **gratitude**, **social connection**, and exercise — (emphasis ours) and said that what is so striking about them "is that they are so simple and accessible. We have become accustomed to thinking that complex problems require complex solutions, but that's not always the case. Sometimes simple solutions can enable us to take on some of our most intractable problems. That's what happiness can do when it comes to health."

The fact that the elements of happiness are being discussed

at all is due in some measure to **Martin Seligman, PhD**, who is commonly known as the founder of **positive psychology** and is the author of multiple best-selling books, beginning with *Learned Helplessness*, and later including *Flourish, Authentic Happiness, Learned Optimism,* and *The Optimistic Child*. You can listen to his TED talk at **https://www.ted.com/talks/martin_seligman_on_the_state_of_psychology?language=en**. His view of psychology—and the view he promoted when he was president of the American Psychological Association—is that "Psychology should be just as concerned with building strength as with repairing damage." Two of the things he has said that resonate most strongly with our views are these:

- *Doing a kindness produces the single most reliable momentary increase in well-being of any exercise we have tested.*

- *When we take time to notice the things that go right—it means we're getting a lot of little rewards throughout the day.*

From Dr. Seligman, we are led to the gratitude work of psychologists, **Dr. Robert A. Emmons** of the University of California, Davis, and **Dr. Michael E. McCullough** of the University of Miami. Dr. Emmons is the author of *Gratitude Works!: A 21-Day Program for Creating Emotional Prosperity* and *Thanks!: How Practicing Gratitude Can Make You Happier*. He is also the founding editor-in-chief of The Journal of Positive Psychology, and defines gratitude as

> *"a felt sense of wonder, thankfulness, and appreciation for life."*

That's the state of mind we hope you find yourself in.

> *Gratitude is a sort of laughter of the heart.*
> — DAVID BROOKS, COLUMNIST

When it comes to **humor**, the list of academic researchers and amusing practitioners is long, and seems best left to our Resources section. However, one resource worth pointing out is the book authored by cognitive neuroscientist **Scott Weems, PhD**: *Ha!: The Science of When We Laugh and Why*. He said:

When we refer to someone as having a humorous personality, what we mean is that this person sees the ambiguity, confusion, and strife inherent in life and turns them into pleasure.

What could be more delightful than that?

Finally, humor leads us to play, and our favorite expert for this topic is **Stuart Brown, MD**, the author of *Play: How it Shapes the Brain, Opens the Imagination and Invigorates the Soul*. He says, what may be the most important quote of all:

"I don't think it is too much to say that play can save your life. It certainly has salvaged mine. Life without play is a grinding, mechanical existence organized around doing the things necessary for survival. Play is the stick that stirs the drink. It is the basis of all art, games, books, sports, movies, fashion, fun, and wonder—in short, the basis of what we think of as civilization. Play is the vital essence of life. It is what makes life lively."

"YOUR NEW PACEMAKER COMES WITH PANDORA SO YOU CAN ALWAYS HAVE A SONG IN YOUR HEART."

Cartoons provided by Glasbergen Cartoon Service

A summary of how gratitude, humor, and play are connected

In short, gratitude, humor, and play are *connected*. Compare these condensed lists of their benefits. Do you see how they intertwine?

GRATITUDE CAN:

- Foster greater happiness, a more hopeful outlook, more positive emotions and fewer negative feelings such as anger, envy, depression, loneliness, and anxiety
- Help us savor life, live in the present
- Strengthen relationships by building social bonds as we become more helpful, empathetic to others
- Increase energy
- Reduce stress
- Boost our immune system, lower blood pressure and reduce inflammation
- Facilitate communication, interrupt aggression
- Create a positive atmosphere in which to work/live

> *At times our own light goes out and is rekindled by a spark from another person. Each of us has cause to think with deep gratitude of those who have lighted the flame within us.*
>
> — ALBERT SCHWEITZER

HUMOR CAN:

- Increase energy
- Reduce stress
- Boost the immune system
- Boost brain power by triggering new connections, finding

new solutions

- Enhance creativity
- Facilitate communication, interrupt aggression, diffuse conflict
- Strengthen relationships by building trust and a climate of cooperation
- Create an optimal environment for working/learning/living

> *Like a welcome summer rain, humor may suddenly cleanse and cool the earth, the air and you.*
>
> — LANGSTON HUGHES

PLAY CAN:

- Refresh your mind and body/increase energy
- Improve brain function and boost creativity
- Improve relationships and your connection to others—encourage teamwork and cooperation.
- Change perspective and help you see problems in new ways
- Create a positive atmosphere in which to work/live

> *Play is the answer to the question, "How does anything new come about?"*
>
> — JEAN PIAGET

So how can you nurture these elements?

If social networks are the key to wellbeing, nurturing relationships is obviously essential. It begins with *acknowledging* the value of those people in your life—expressing gratitude, because when you openly value others, your friendship circle grows.

Gratitude facilitates communication

Another benefit of expressing gratitude is that it sets the tone for positive communication.

- When you are approached by someone who looks angry, greet her with a compliment (something you appreciate about her): *"Good morning, Mrs. Jones. What a beautiful sweater you're wearing!"*

- When you are criticized by a parent or peer, begin by thanking him for the insight he has given you: *"Thank you for telling me; I didn't know that was how you understood what happened,"* (or indeed what really happened or how he felt about what happened).

Gratitude interrupts aggression and restarts the conversation.

Gratitude creates a positive atmosphere

Positive words permeate the atmosphere like a pleasant perfume wafting through the air. When you walk into a room, you can instantly recognize whether the atmospheric charge is negative (tense) or positive (welcoming). You help to make it welcoming with your words and actions. If you are leading a meeting, class, or an activity, add gratitude to the openings and closings and provide abundant affirmation:

- Greetings: Start each meeting by saying, *"I'm so grateful you're here."*

- Farewells: End each meeting by saying something like, *"I'm so glad we had this time together."*

- In meetings and throughout the day look for ways to offer individual praise: *"I love coming in each day and seeing your smiling face."*

> *"I've learned that people will forget what you said, people will forget what you did, but people will never forget how you made them feel."*
>
> — MAYA ANGELOU

Note that what we have said for gratitude works equally well when you add humor and play to your repertoire.

Creating the rituals

Chief rule: Variety is the spice of life. Most gratitude rituals are best if practiced for only a limited time. They can be repeated eventually, but move on to something new every week or two, because, for example, if you leave a particular "gratitude tree" sample up for more than two weeks, you will see it has become part of the furniture — ignored and taken for granted rather than continuing to create delight. Humor and play tend to have the same effect. You can show a cartoon every day to a class of students, but you cannot show the same cartoon or they will soon doubt your sanity. Similarly, three-year olds can play the same game endlessly (Candyland, anyone?) but the rest of us want variety. Keep that in mind as you review the possibilities in the next chapters.

A footnote:

While we have been writing this book, the Dalai Lama and Desmond Tutu, with authorship assistance from Douglas Abrams, have come out with *The Book of Joy: Lasting Happiness in a Changing World*. Developed from a five-day conversation in 2015 between the Dalai Lama and Tutu, Archbishop Emeritus of South Africa, on the occasion of the Dalai Lama's 80th birthday, it focuses on cultivating wellbeing through their "eight pillars of joy." These pillars are perspective, humility, humor, acceptance, forgiveness, gratitude, compassion, and generosity. What we are trying to do through our book is provide some practical and pleasant ways to practice those pillars.

Chapter 2

Giving and Receiving Compliments

Compliments are the helium that fills everyone's balloon; they elevate the person receiving them so he or she can fly over life's troubles and land safely on the other side.

— BERNIE SIEGEL

We are giving this brief topic its own chapter, because it is really the foundation for the next two chapters about being specific in expressing our gratitude.

One of the key elements of creating an atmosphere of gratitude is through the abundant bestowing of compliments, but in our experience, most people are lousy at giving and accepting them. Too many people tend to give superficial praise, and on the receiving end, too many tend to deflect the importance of that praise, thinking they are being modest.

Also in our experience, men have a harder time giving good compliments, in part because they tend to focus on the physical and then open themselves up to accusations of sexual harassment. On the other hand, women tend to be poor receivers. When a man says, *"That's a pretty dress,"* he should not be immediately suspected of ulterior motives, and a woman should not negate the compliment by saying, *"This old thing? I've had it for years, and just dragged it out of the back of the closet because I was too tired to do the laundry last night."*

Here are the rules for giving and receiving compliments. It may be awkward at first, but practice makes perfect.

How to give a compliment

- Be specific. *"Nice shirt,"* doesn't cut it. Try, *"Wow, the color of your blouse really brings out the color in your eyes!"*

- Acknowledge character over appearance. *"You were really kind to Mrs. Jones yesterday. I admire you for that."*

- Be sincere. Don't say it if you don't mean it. Flattery falls flat.

- Be appreciative. *"Your sense of humor lightened the tough situation I was in with Principal Smith today. I'm grateful to you for intervening."*

Note that acknowledging *character* is about admiring *who someone is*; being appreciative is acknowledging *what someone did*.

When you admire a person's appearance, that can be a confidence booster for the moment, but when you admire someone's character, it's as good in the days ahead as it was when the person was wearing her eye-enhancing blouse. Similarly, when you show appreciation for a helpful action, you encourage more of those kinds of actions, bringing out the best in that person well beyond the day of your compliment.

Chapter 2

How to accept a compliment

A compliment is a gift; accept it graciously, and *never* reject it. If you reject my gift, you are depriving me of the pleasure I have in giving it, depriving yourself of the pleasure I intended for you, and calling my taste or judgment into question. When I compliment you on something you describe as *"This old thing,"* I feel foolish. A rejected compliment can make us both feel bad when the intention in giving it was to make both of us feel good!

When given a compliment, smile, make eye contact, and simply say, **"Thank you."** If you must add more, try:

- *That's very nice of you to say.*

- *It means a lot to me to hear that from you.*

- *I like this scarf, too. It was a gift from a good friend.*

- *It was my pleasure to be helpful.*

- *I'm so glad my hard work paid off.*

Note also that you diminish the pleasure of the sincere giver of a compliment when you immediately turn it around and say, *"Oh, but I love your dress, too."* Don't assume the other person is fishing for a compliment of his or her own. Bask in the moment of pleasure the compliment-giver intended for you.

The exception, as anyone who has witnessed an awards ceremony can attest, is that it is poor form to take all the credit for anything that was a group effort. In that case, say something like: *"Thank you. I want you to know your help was invaluable; I couldn't have done this without your support."*

That's how toasts work, too. If you are lucky enough to be the guest of honor at a dinner and the host welcomes you warmly with a toast, the proper response is to smile, nod, raise your glass, and when everyone has taken a sip, respond in kind. *"Thank you, Mr. Jones, for your kind words and this lovely gathering. I feel honored to be here."*

Bottom line: Creating an atmosphere of gratitude begins with kind words spoken with sincerity to one another. Everyone in your organization, school, family, or other setting has a role to play in atmosphere creation, and yet it costs nothing and can produce enormous returns in wellbeing. Commit to it, and you will find a positively charged (and changed) place.

> *Feeling gratitude and not expressing it is like wrapping a present and not giving it.*
>
> ~ William Arthur Ward

Chapter 3

Visual varieties of creating expressions of delight and gratitude

In our visual world, creating a visual version of appreciation is both fun and open to infinite varieties of expression. In this section we are introducing you to a few of them.

To keep our wording simple, we are calling almost all of our examples "gratitude trees," although they take many other forms, and, as you will see, can be used to express many messages beyond gratitude.

The first decision to make related to your visual version is, "Will it be indoors or out?"

Outdoor gratitude trees

First of all, outdoor gratitude trees are appealing because:

- They provide a reason for people to go outside into fresh air and linger there.

- They immediately bring to mind gratitude for the beauty of nature.

- In cold climates during winter, they provide a bright spot in a bare landscape.

The possibilities for what to make a focal point are limited only by what's in your garden. In our samples, we used a wall of ivy, leafless trees, a flowering bush, and a lavender bush. Generally, we suggest using foliage that is easy for participants to reach, which means bushes may be better than trees for children and older adults. Reachability is important not only for hanging the messages, but also for making it easy for those who stop by to read those messages. You don't want people to injure themselves stretching up too high or stooping down too low. Also keep in mind that the ground around the foliage should be flat and stable. Another alternative? Look for ways to use these ideas in a raised garden bed.

Our only other guidelines for outdoor gratitude trees are these:

- Use biodegradable materials like paper and yarn or string that birds might be able to recycle.

- You can use white paper on a green bush in summer, but aim for colorful paper and yarn if this is a winter activity on bare branches.

Chapter 3

Example 1: Yellow flowers

We chose a leafy green bush that would soon have yellow flowers of its own for our first outdoor gratitude tree, and covered it with yellow construction paper flower shapes. The names of the people on the flowers represent "those who have helped us blossom" into the people we are today.

Example 2: Colorful hearts

Hearts are one of the easiest designs to cut out, and while they look lovely in a simple combination of pinks and reds, on this bare Japanese lily tree, we thought a full range of colors was in order. Hearts, of course, can list the people we love, but can also be used as a catchall for virtually anything we love—pets, places, possessions, for example. Or you can make the topic multi-sensory—sights, sounds, touches, fragrances you love.

Example 3: Purple noses on lavender

Speaking of fragrances, a lavender bush seemed like the perfect place to hang purple noses that highlighted smells that we enjoy, from a baby's skin to baking bread. Coming up with a design for noses was a little tricky, but we really could have used any shape at all.

Example 4: Musical notes on ivy

This dense wall of green ivy created a great contrast for our black and white musical notes and keyboards. We see two main ways you can use these symbols: list people or things that make your heart sing, or list the types of music you enjoy or particular songs or musicians that are significant for you.

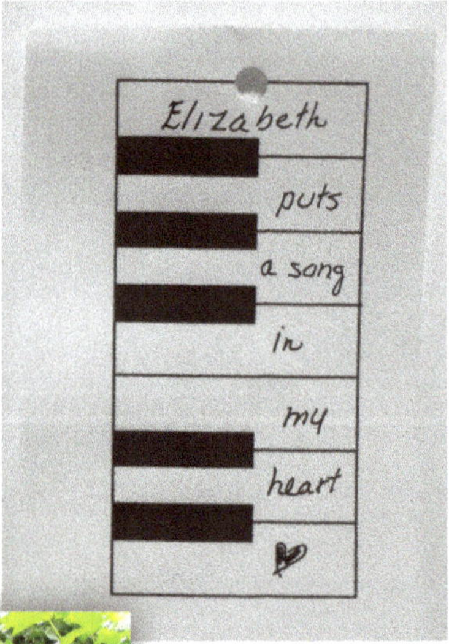

Example 5: Create a garden path

We used very inexpensive plastic plates that could be cut into flowery shapes, wrote on them with permanent markers, and added stickers. We found some colorful, very long plastic straws to use as sticks and added construction paper green leaves, to the straw stems, but soon found that the straws were too flimsy and needed reinforcement; we would recommend dowels instead. For picture purposes, we lined up the paper plates close together, but a nicer variation might be to place 20 or more at wide intervals along a walking trail or near resting benches along the way. Another variation would be to group them all together in a large ceramic outdoor pot.

Example 6: Spirals on a tree

Spirals make a particularly appealing message to hang on a tree because they spin with the slightest breeze (as you can see in the video on our website at www.CreatingDelight.com). We hung our samples on low-hanging bare branches in winter which made them especially spin-able. Plus, as our example illustrates, you can write more than a name on a spiral. You can write a whole story about something that pleases you. This is one activity that is very likely to go over well with children, making it perfect for intergenerational gatherings.

Chapter 3

Indoor variations

If outdoor gratitude trees are limited perhaps by the foliage in your garden, indoor trees are limited only by your imagination.

Let's start by looking at examples using dried plant materials, but keep in mind that you can just as easily use a real indoor potted plant such as a ficus. Our dried materials came from an Australian chain store called Spotlight, but you might also find a wide variety from Lincraft or almost any two dollar shop. In the U.S., check out dollar stores, Michael's and Jo-Ann Fabrics.

For all of the following examples we rotated the use of these batches of foliage materials:

- Some dried, spirally, straw-like red sticks
- A tall bare branch that was actually made of paper and wire
- 2 red and 2 green eucalyptus branches
- A packet of dried seed pods, spiral leaves, and interesting green stuff
- A plastic green branch with red berries on it

Example 1: Circles 1

Circles, of course, are one of the easiest and most pleasing shapes to cut out and write on. In this example, we used a combination of plain blue and green circles and circles cut out from wrapping paper. The wrapping paper circles were folded at the top so the message could be written on the plain inside. The plain blue and green circles could have messages written on one or both sides; they could also be created with a fold and an inside message, allowing for decoration on the outside. Wrapping paper, with its huge range of variations, provides endless color and pattern possibilities. For our foliage, we stuck solidly to green as most aesthetically pleasing for this combination. We might also have made the circles into "ornaments" for December holidays. Really, any message with any theme can be written on circles; see our metaphor list at the end of this section.

Example 2: Circles 2

Next, we changed out our dried plant materials and added multi-colored circles that we had decorated with a variety of stickers. We tied them on with almost transparent blue ribbon for a subtle effect. We also considered making our circles into oranges, cherries or other round fruits or baseballs, cricket balls, golf, soccer, and other sport balls.

Example 3: Birds on a tree

Birds seem an ideal image for trees, and lend themselves well to messages about sounds of nature you are grateful for, people or animals that cheer you up, people who are the wind beneath your wings, or just a list of birds that you especially like. We gave our birds whimsical shapes and googly eyes.

Example 4: Candles on a tree

We made our candles out of glitter paper (which has a white back side for easily writing messages) and construction paper "flames," then hung them on our tree with gold loops. Candles can also symbolize many joys: people who light up your life or who have led you out of darkness, or even something ordinary like inventions that make your life brighter.

Example 5: Hanging notecards

Here's one way to use the spirally red stuff. We bought a set of 10 very inexpensive notecards in a charity shop and essentially cut them in half, punched a hole in the corner and hung them directly on the spirals. Because they are notecards, they were already folded and ready for a message to be written inside.

Chapter 3

Example 6: Spoons attached to cards

A simple little plastic green branch with red berries found in a two dollar shop formed the basis for this tree expressing gratitude for foods we love. We found the tiny plastic silver spoons in the party section of a discount store and attached them to pink tags (representing our tongues) that listed favorite foods suggested to us.

Example 7: Black thingamajig

Bron found this item in a craft shop. It's like the spokes on an umbrella if they were made of a completely flexible (floppy) black plastic material. When held upright, they flop about, perfect to hang messages on. When it is held upside down, the "spokes" collapse into a long, thin entity that fits easily into a mailing tube for storage. We don't know if you can find anything like it, but take this simply as advice to look at odd objects in new ways.

Chapter 3

Indoor gratitude trees that aren't multi-dimensional trees

Gratitude messages can also hang on a wall.

As we noted earlier, no visual version of gratitude should be on display for longer than two weeks because it quickly becomes ignored as just part of the furniture. That means that creating visuals that can be easily put up and taken down and recycled for use another time should be a priority.

Example 1: Create a wall-hanging

We created our tree by first folding a white plastic tablecloth in half. It can be hung in whatever way works best in your situation that will not damage walls. One of the simplest ways is to stretch a cord between the tablecloth fold and secure it at both ends.

We created our greenery by taking a light green plastic tablecloth (both tablecloths are easy to find at a dollar store), again folding it, cutting it into a fluffy foliage cloud shape and gluing it to the white table cloth. We doubled it up to create a stronger color base, but you might not need to do so if you use a darker color.

We took black poster board to make the tree trunk and what we hope looks like random branches sticking through the green foliage.

To illustrate a few of the possible uses for this tree, we then

- recycled our outdoor yellow blossoms,
- cut out a variety of leaf shapes in fall colors, and
- added red and pink hearts.

We could also have used our birds or circles, or for that matter, any other shape we chose. The idea is to create something that draws our eye and entices us to stop and read.

Chapter 3

Example 2: Frame a poster

You can also create smaller wall hangings by using poster board and framing it. Since space is limited on poster board, this works best for families or small groups, but an alternative is to group three or four posters together on a wall.

For our first poster example, we took **butterfly** cut-outs purchased at an art supply store, wrote on the underside of the wings, and glued the middle body to a sky blue poster. As you can see from the example, we used the metaphors of soaring (people who have helped you soar) and, as with the birds, people who have been the wind beneath your wings.

Next, we took **white stars** and put them on a glittery black poster board with messages about the people who brighten your life or who have been the inspiring stars in your life. You can also take a more lighthearted approach and simply have people write down the celebrities they admire.

By adding **red stars** and switching to a glittery blue background, a patriotic theme seems obvious that celebrates independence, veterans, freedoms you enjoy, etc.

Chapter 3

Another use for the black glittery poster board is as a background to the **candles** we put on an indoor tree in the earlier example. They can list the people who light up your life, who brighten the path and lead the way. They can also simply list anyone with a birthday that month.

One note about candles as messages: They work as well outdoors as in, but don't use glittery paper outdoors, because it is not as biodegradable as construction or other paper.

Note: While we have provided close-ups of possible messages, many of our illustrations do not show how the tree looks with visible messages. We purposely left them off so that you could see the beauty of the overall creation. Whether to show messages is up to you. Virtually all can be hidden by writing on the back side of the shape you use or by creating designs with a fold and writing the message inside. How visible you want or need the messages to be is up to you.

Example 3: Hang bunting

The festive triangles on a string that are used as hanging decorations for many occasions come in a wide variety of colors and patterns. For our sample, we used a prepackaged version from a party store, but substituted a sparkly blue mesh ribbon for the string that came with it.

For any hanging banner you use, the theme can be related to whatever holiday you are celebrating, or to whatever way you are "hanging in there" or whatever you are "hanging around for."

Example 4: Hang a wreath

We first used a Styrofoam wreath covered in folded leaves with messages on the inside to show you how you can change a base for the seasons—**spring leaves,** then **fall leaves**.

We then used the wreath covered in **hands** to show how the circle shape can serve other purposes, in this case, people who have lent a helping hand.

There are many other possibilities for shapes on wreaths.

Example 5: Make a whimsical bird

We wanted to do something completely different, so inspired by an idea for a Thanksgiving turkey, we made a whimsical bird with tail feathers that list the "animals that make me laugh." We wound two Styrofoam balls in yarn, joined them with toothpicks, then added a paper beak and googly eyes. We stuck some colorful real feathers at the back end of the larger ball just for show. Then we wrote the names of animals whose antics amuse us on construction paper "feathers," taped those feathers to toothpicks, and stuck them just in front of the real feathers.

What we didn't do is figure out the feet, so we propped our bird in a shallow bowl for her photo. We could have shaved off one side of the larger Styrofoam ball so that the bird had a flat, stable bottom. Alternatively, we could have created feet from Play-doh or a similar substance.

Example 6: Make an apple

Who are the people who are the apple of your eye? Write their names on each end of 4 strips of red or green paper. Then glue or staple the strips in a circle. Bring all the ends together at the top and staple again. Add a little leaf to cover the staple, and now you have your very own reminder of the people you care most about.

If we were to do this over, we would use thinner, longer strips and lighter weight paper.

The shapes of the messages

One of the reasons you can use the same foliage over and over again for your gratitude trees is that you can change the shape of the messages that you hang on them multiple times.

Pre-cut shapes

You can purchase packages of many pre-cut shapes from office supply, teacher supply, and craft stores as we did for our butterflies, handprints, footprints, and boomerangs, for example. Many other paper and foam shapes are available. If you find a shape you want to use, this will save a lot of cutting and enable participants to concentrate on decorating those shapes. But both cutting and decorating can be pleasant group exercises in themselves. Very young children and older adults with arthritic hands may find cutting difficult, but that leaves a wide range of people in between.

Templates

A wide variety of shapes are also available online for downloading. To save you time, **we have created a packet available free on our website when you register your email.**

Note that there are two types of templates. The first is a simple outline of a star, circle or heart, for example, that can be copied and cut out multiple times in various sizes and decorated or left plain. A circle, as we noted above, can become an ornament or a soccer ball or an orange, among many other possibilities.

The second type of template is more detailed. It can be filled in with a variety of colors making for an interesting art project of its own.

A third alternative is to cut out a square or rectangle that the shape is printed on and use that as your template — cutting is then minimized. That worked well for us with musical notes and keyboards.

Make your own shape

The directions for an origami shirt came from Activity Connection. (See our website: **www.CreatingDelight.com**) We like it because a message can be written on the outside or on a piece of paper slipped into the pocket formed between the collar and the back of the shirt. Shirts can lend themselves to a masculine theme or to recognizing the men in your life whom you have reason to appreciate. Other origami designs are also possible message conveyors.

Chapter 3

We wanted to make a **tie shape**, again as a shape related to masculinity, and found many possible templates online, but chose to make ours shorter and wider, in order to fit more into a smaller space. Wrapping paper would have been an easy choice for finding likely tie designs, but we had purchased a packet of Mexican fiesta-style paper on sale and chose to use samples of that instead.

Creating Delight

We used that same packet of paper to make **paper fans**. Because of the folds, messages need to be written on a separate piece of paper and taped to the back side, but the theme can cover a wide range of people, events, and things that you are a fan of.

You'll find many more ideas under our metaphor list.

Chapter 3

Notecards, bookmarks, scrapbook supplies, sticky notes and more

As we scoured clearance racks, discount stores, and charity shops, we found many other paper-based ideas that messages of delight could be written on.

- Sticky notes of socks made us feel warm and cozy, so perhaps that's a suitable theme for them: What else makes you feel warm and cozy?

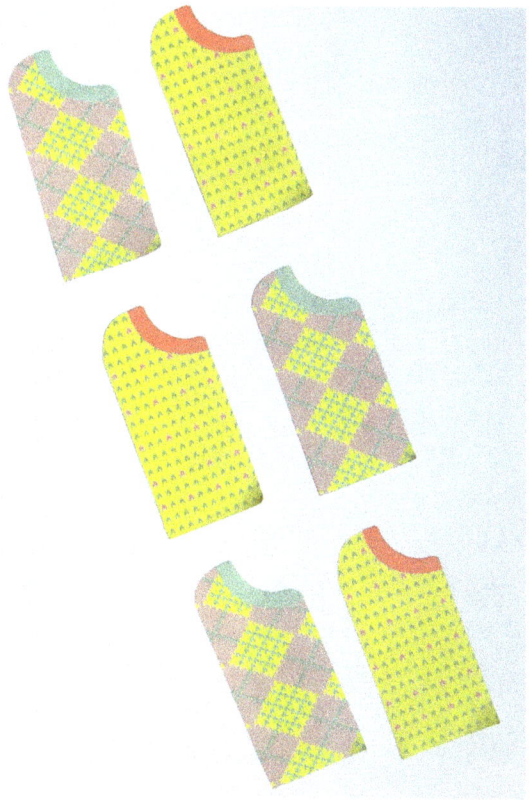

- Sticky notes of **cupcakes** are obviously for all the sweets that please you.

- We found colorful oversized sheets with a variety of messages intended for scrapbooking projects, but that were easily cut up to use here instead.

- One of these sheets included days of the week, especially great for daily gratitude.

- We found bookmarks and book plates, place setting cards, gift tags, and small notecards.

- As described in the next chapter, we also found many beautiful journaling cards. These are from Project Life, but there are many other vendors. They can be used on any visual version for creating delight that needs to be done quickly — i.e., time for writing messages, but no time for participants to make their own cards.

Chapter 3

Other props

While we were able to incorporate the plastic **silver spoons** with favorite things to eat, we didn't find workable uses for everything we gathered. Here are some of the ideas that remained incomplete at press time. Can you do better?

- We wanted to tie colorful plastic **swizzle sticks** to glittery paper with messages about the "people we would gladly drink a toast to," but the result of our efforts was not eye-catching.

- We wanted to do something with small **shells** glued to paper with a sandy background (or possibly even sand paper), but got bogged down with indecision because we thought it would also be neat to create a little sandbox and put real or paper shells in that.

- We found clothespins in the shape of **fish** and thought of tying a bunch of strings to a makeshift bamboo fishing pole with a fish at the end of each string. Each fish would have a note clipped to it that said, "Dropping you a line…" to which participants could add their own messages. For example, "To the events committee: Dropping you a line to say thanks for the help with the ice cream social last week."

- We found regular **clothespins** in a wide variety of sizes and colors, and thought of creating a clothesline with the shapes of various clothing items clipped to them. Our dilemma? What should the message theme be and could we make a clothesline look aesthetically pleasing?

Do these ideas generate more ideas for you? We hope so!

Chapter 3

A few guidelines for visual versions

Vases/containers—For the purposes of this book, we used almost exclusively a single white ceramic vase that cost well under $10. For workshops, where multiple vases are needed, we have turned to a dollar store to purchase plastic (i.e., unbreakable) vases and those colored marble-like stones to weight the bottom and minimize the likelihood of it tipping. Tipping can also be minimized by buying vases with a wider base than top. If the vase is opaque, you can fill the vase with plastic bags or florists' foam to position the stems of your foliage. One advantage of the inexpensive vases: We have found that some people like to decorate their vases using the same theme as they use for their tree.

Fake foliage—As noted elsewhere, we are partial to real plant material that has been dried or treated, such as various wood products, seed pods, pussy willows, eucalyptus leaves, and even bare branches brought in from the outdoors. All of these can be found in craft stores (even the bare branches). But that said,

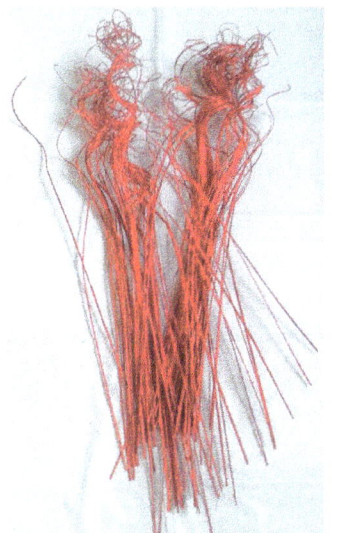

in our workshops, we have offered the choice of fake foliage covered in a variety of leaves and blossoms, and found that some people like white flowers to set off the colorful message tags they use, and others like, for example, yellow flowers to enhance a yellow and green spring theme they have chosen. To be honest, we've found all of them aesthetically pleasing and believe it's best to be flexible.

Tying the message on—Here are some of the possibilities:

- Wrapping paper ribbon and other decorative ribbon or narrow lace
- Yarn
- Colorful string/thin rope
- Colorful clothespins (various sizes or shapes)
- Pipe cleaners
- Raffia

Paper—There's an infinite range of possibilities here, but we have found that sticking to a color theme is most pleasing to the eye. If you are using a pattern, it's often more appealing to add some message tags in a plain color that matches one or more of the colors in the pattern. In doing so, however, especially if you are working with older adults, be sure to use light colors or the white back side (or folded inside) for your messages. Black pen on a red or dark green paper, for example, will be hard for many older adults to read. If a pattern or color is only printed on one side of the paper, you might want to create folded tags and write on the white interior. For tags that require multiple folds, make sure the paper is lightweight and easy to manipulate.

Chapter 3

Pens and writing utensils—We are big believers in using washable markers. They are easy for young and old to use and don't make a mess (and if they do, can be cleaned up easily). Crayon doesn't easily create the same solid lines and are too childish for older adults. That said, permanent markers may be better for outdoor tree projects. Some people like using ballpoint or artist pens. Others like cutting out the words for their message from magazines. One caution regarding markers: Any colors can be used for decorating the message tags, but the message itself needs to be written in black or another color that provides strong contrast to the tag's background, such as dark green, blue, or purple.

The primary goal is to make the message legible, and for that, it may be necessary to have participants dictate their thoughts, type them into a computer, and print them out in a large, clean font that can be glued to the message tag. This is especially likely if participants are very young or very old and cannot write as legibly as needed.

Stickers and other enhancements—Stickers are everywhere and come in infinite varieties. They are one of the easiest ways to decorate your own tags, but don't hesitate to use any other sort of enhancements you wish. Consider, for example, watercolors, decoupage or collage designs, adding lace or fabric, or creating a Zentangle design as we did with the footprint sample. We added spoons to one set of message tags, and you can find many other ideas in the party section of any store or in the scrapbooking or rubber stamp area of any craft store. See both the Resources section of this book and our website, **www.CreatingDelight.com,** for more ideas.

Chapter 3

Visual versions resources

We feel strongly that whatever form your gratitude tree takes, it should be visually appealing, adding eye-catching color and beauty to the room or the outdoor space it occupies.

At the same time, we are bargain hunters. With regard to all the supplies purchased for this book and our workshops, we looked for "tree material" that could be reused multiple times, and tried to purchase quality materials at discounted prices.

In terms of the paper materials used for writing messages, we sought out every source we could, including:

- Our own supply cabinets and stationery stashes

- Inexpensive notecards, bookmarks, stickers, and other materials that looked promising at flea markets, church rummage sales, and in charity shops

- Loads of $2 shops (Australia) and dollar shops (U.S.)

- Clearance items in craft, art, party, and office supply stores

- Asking families and friends for their leftovers

If you are creating a gratitude tree as a one-time activity for your school, senior center or other location, finding these materials can be time-consuming, but easily adequate, especially if you have a particular seasonal theme in mind. Plus, if you reach out to family and friends or the likely participants themselves, you are likely to gain their enthusiastic involvement even before you begin.

If you need supplies for a group of people who are making gratitude trees as individuals or teams and need to buy items in quantity, see the Resources section for more ideas.

Metaphors by shape

As all our samples of visual versions for creating delight show, choosing a theme is easily enhanced by using metaphors and creating visuals and messages with the metaphor in mind. Following are the metaphors we used for the samples in this book, and more we might have added. Also, as we have noted for some of the shapes below, each item can also be taken literally. Flowers may represent the people who have helped you blossom, but it is equally valid for someone to list her favorite kinds of flowers and sign her name on a flower shape.

- **Apple**—People who are the apple of your eye is obvious, but an apple can also represent favorite teachers, or (as in the story of Adam and Eve) curiosity—Name things that stimulate your curiosity and find out who shares your interest.

- **Ball shapes**—These can be related to many topics. Sports balls can be related to favorite sports or teams or individuals on a team. Ornaments can be related to special memories related to December holidays. You might also use orange paper circles for oranges, purple for grapes, red for cherries, and so on, and let the messages be something related to your favorite recipes using fruits (peach cobbler, anyone?) or simply fruits you enjoy. Or simply ask people to choose a color and write, "I love oranges" (or apples, grapes, plums, etc.) and sign their name. Orange circles could also use the theme: "Orange you glad we asked you to name something you love?" Let your imagination out to play!

- **Baseball hats or T-shirt shapes**—Obviously these shapes are good for relating to particular sports and teams, but these days more and more t-shirts and hats are used to provide humorous or philosophical messages, which can be infinitely more interesting.

- **Birds (or just wings)**—These can be about specific birds you like or sounds of nature you are grateful for. Birds tend to cheer us, so think of people who cheer you up or people who are the wind beneath your wings. Another idea is "A little bird told me…" and follow it with a compliment to someone. Or The bluebird of happiness for me is…"

- **Boomerangs**—When has your act of kindness come round back to you?

- **Butterflies**—Things that add beauty to life or things that make you soar or people who have brought you out of your cocoon.

- **Candles**—People who light up your life, provide a light in the darkness, or inventions that make your life brighter/better.

- **Cars**—Although there are women who love their vehicles, our experience is that it is men who will wax nostalgic over their first car or current car or a favorite car. Descriptions of these favorites can be hung on a poster board made to resemble a race track. An alternative can be cars (or planes or trains) that are used to highlight a special trip or favorite place to visit.

- **Cats and dogs**—Or birds or bunnies or any other animal that may have been a beloved pet. Maybe you name and describe this pet, but maybe you also write what you learned from that pet. (Wag your tail whenever you are happy to see someone?)

- **Clams**—What makes you happy as a clam?

- **Corn cob**—Use Indian corn and create paper husks to paste around the bottom. The messages could relate to farmers and what they are grateful for or what you get from farmers that you're appreciative of. Or because it's an "ear" of corn, it could be a person's favorite sounds.

- **Fans**—Who or what are you a fan of? Or who gets you overheated so you have to fan yourself?

- **Fish**—People who've helped you stay in the swim of things? Create a literal game of fishing for compliments? You could also create a big fish and add compliments on "scales." You can also be more literal and simply list favorite fish to catch and/or eat. These ideas might work better for men than some of the "girly" stuff.

- **Flowers**—Things that add beauty to life or people who have helped you blossom.

- **Hands**—Whose helping hands have you been grateful for?

- **Hearts**—People or things you love (Can make it multi-sensory — sights, sounds, touches, fragrances)

- **Leaves**—Because they fit so perfectly on a tree, leaves can be used for any message at all, but you might specifically want to create messages related to things in nature you love or people who have helped you grow.

- **Musical notes or part of a piano keyboard**— Things/people that make your heart sing, your favorite types of music, favorite songs, musicians, singers, etc.

- **Spoons**—Favorite foods: Tie messages on with little plastic (preferably silver) spoons attached. Use these for a tree that is made up of people's favorite foods (I am grateful for chocolate, etc.), for favorite types of food (comfort food, vegetables, desserts, etc.), or for listing the people who feed your soul.

- **Stars**—Can be people who light up your life, make your life brighter, or people you admire (celebrities, heroes) or who have served their country in some way (when used for a patriotic holiday)

- **Sparkly/glittery** messages in any shape — People or things that dazzle you or make your life brighter in some way. As noted earlier, you might list inventions in this category, for example.

Creating Delight

- **Smiley faces**—People or things that make you smile or laugh. But note that there are other ways to highlight this idea as when we created a whimsical yarn bird and gave her paper tail feathers each with the name of creatures that amuse us (otters, ducks, monkeys).

- **Swizzle sticks**—Attach these to messages as things you will toast/drink to

- **Shells**—Use these metaphorically as people who have either protected you (created a shell around you) in times of trouble or who have led you out of your shell into a wider world. More literally, you can simply list things you love about the sea, or your favorite beaches.

- **Umbrellas**—When have you let your smile be your umbrella? When have you felt like singing in the rain?

- **Watermelon**—This can be literally things that remind you of summer fun or favorite summer fruits. Because traditionally watermelon has prominent black seeds, it can also serve as a metaphor for the people who have provided the seeds of an idea that changed you in some way—provided direction, helped you grow.

Note: A word about favorites

It's common for us to say things like, "What's your favorite color?" Some people can tell you instantly, but others of us like many colors, and will hesitate to pick just one. The same may be true for foods, vacation spots, movie stars, and many other categories. To overcome that hesitation, consider using different wording, such as, "What are some of the colors you especially like?" or "If you could transport yourself to anywhere in the world right now, where would you like to be?" The idea is to generate lots of ideas in people, not just one.

More ideas for topics that can be visually illustrated

As noted earlier, we have used the term "gratitude tree" as a catchall for the ideas in this section, but because this book is about humor and play and anything that can produce delight, following are a few other ideas for themes for creating visual delight on any sort of "tree" using any shape you choose. Don't be limited by the suggestions here. *Do* use them to jumpstart your thinking.

People—Who has made your life richer? In each case, name the specific person, and if possible, give a brief explanation of why

- Friends
- Family/relatives
- Teachers
- Mentors/leaders
- Artists/authors/musicians/ composers
- Authors/poets
- Moral or spiritual leaders
- Innovators/inventors
- Health care workers

Creating Delight

This sculpture by Claes Oldenburg and Coosje Van Brugeen is found in the gardens of the Walker Art Center, Minneapolis, MN, USA.

Use the ideas from others to expand your knowledge of artists, authors, musicians, etc. That can be a delight of its own!

Also, you can go back to family and friends again and again if you are specific:

- Use clocks as your symbol and answer: What have they done for you over time? (May or may not have been appreciated AT the time)

- What have they done today or recently that has pleased you?

- What do you like or admire about them?

- With regard to grandparents talking about grandchildren or teachers talking about students, what are the funny or insightful things they have said?

Inventors and innovators can also lead us to:
- Inventions and conveniences (things you couldn't live without)
- Luxuries you love to be pampered with

Examples: Conveniences
- Central heat and AC
- Bowls and spoons
- Jar openers
- Deodorant
- Lipstick
- Toilet paper

Examples: Appreciated inventions
- Eye glasses and hearing aids
- Computers and spell check
- Paper, ink, books
- Microwave oven
- Dishwashers
- Sticky notes
- Zippers

Tune into your senses:
Examples: Tastes—Comfort food
- Brownies or favorite chocolate
- Mac and cheese
- Ice cream
- Popcorn
- Pizza

Creating Delight

Examples: Smells
- Coffee brewing
- Bread baking
- Lilacs in spring
- Rain
- Baby's skin
- Sunscreen

Examples: Sights
- Toddlers at the beach
- Your favorite movie star
- A flowering garden
- Anything that sparkles
- Campfire
- Color!

Examples: Sounds
- Your favorite singer or musician playing your favorite music
- Fall leaves crunching beneath your feet
- The voice of a beloved friend or relative
- Children laughing
- Wine cork popping

Examples: Touch—Things that feel good
- The just-right pillow beneath your head
- Fuzzy socks and comfy underwear
- Shawl on shoulders
- Hugs, and hands held

- A good night's sleep
- The sun's warmth
- Toes in soft sand
- Soft grass

Luxuries and things you love to do

Note that even if the topic isn't specifically "Things I am grateful for," thinking of something that pleases you, such as luxuries you love to be pampered with (back rub, fragrant flowers, a pedicure) will conjure up its own pleasure—a bit of delight.

Examples: Oddities and luxuries—What's the most unusual thing you are grateful for?

- Water in all its forms (including oceans)
- Manicures and pedicures
- Recipes that turn out right
- Salt and other spices
- Good hair days
- Libraries
- Gravity

Examples: Things you love to do

- Gardening or flower arranging
- Playing with a pet
- Reading
- Painting
- Needlework
- Any hobby

What else delights you?

Consider a theme of things that make you laugh, such as:

- Your favorite uncle's /grandchild's jokes
- Inadvertently funny signs
- Cat videos
- Puns

What else makes you laugh or smile or simply amuses you? Could you have a joke tree?

Sample messages

If the topic is favorite desserts, most people can come up with multiple possibilities, but if the topic is something I appreciate about someone — especially because in our pages about compliments we have said it's important to be specific — some people need a jumpstart. Following are a few ideas for students and teachers and older adults and their carers.

Older adults might appreciate in their specific carers:

- Their gentle touch when arthritis causes pain
- Patience, not hurrying me
- Pushing me to keep exercising
- Listening to my worries

The carers might appreciate in specific older residents their:

- Resilient spirit
- Patience when I am clumsy in my care
- Determination even when it seems like stubbornness in the moment
- Bright smile when I know you may not feel like smiling

Senior settings—Administrators might appreciate in specific staff:

- How you put your knowledge to work
- That you see the individual before the task
- Your reliability when I know it isn't easy to be/get here

Senior settings—Administrators or staff might appreciate specific family members for:

- Sharing what has worked for you in caring for your family member
- Sharing your loved one's biography now that she no longer can do so herself
- Your help with the botanical garden outing (or any other help)

Teachers might appreciate in specific students:

- Perseverance
- A curious mind
- A quick wit even when it is sometimes disruptive
- A willingness to try

Students might appreciate in their teachers:

- Your faith in my abilities even when I've lost my own
- Your patience when I find a concept hard to understand
- Your ability to make learning fun
- Your leadership in showing how everyone has value

Chapter 4
Additional creating delight rituals

As we noted earlier, variety is the spice of life. Rituals for creating delight are best if practiced for only a limited time. They can be repeated eventually, but move on to something new every week or two to keep your enthusiasm fresh.

On the following pages are a variety of exercises, many related specifically to gratitude, that you might try for adding delight to your setting. As resources, we used our experiences, imagination, a variety of books, and ideas from friends. We also scoured the Internet, and while many people repeated the same ideas, credit should be given specifically to Marelisa Fabrega, who in 2012 wrote this **http://daringtolivefully.com/gratitude-exercises**, and some of whose ideas you will see reflected below.

1) Morning coffee or tea gratitude

Some people start the day with meditation or prayer, which is usually a form of gratitude of its own, but even if you have only a minute or two as you grab a cup of coffee or tea, you can take in the moment and appreciate:

- The warmth of the mug
- The aroma

- The first sip
- The new day and its anticipated joys (not just its obligations)
- Anything else you can think of, including when true, the luxury of a slow start

2) Grace before meals

For some, this is a religious ritual that comes naturally, but you don't have to be religious to appreciate the farmers, the grocers, the cooks, the servers, and the nourishment the meal provides. Here's a non-religious grace found at http://secularseasons.org/celebrations/graces.html:

> *For the meal we are about to eat,*
> *For those who made it possible,*
> *And for those with whom we are about to share it,*
> *We are thankful.*

You can, of course, also write your own, or ask others in your group to do so. Brevity is appreciated, but so is reminding people of something specific such as:

We are thankful for that glorious concert of birds singing this morning or *We are grateful that Mrs. Jones shared her brownie recipe with our cooks and that they have chosen to make it for today's dessert.* Every pleasant thought conjured by one person and shared, conjures positive thoughts in all who hear it.

3) A late-in-the-day gratitude and delight idea

I have long encouraged residential care settings to hold a late afternoon "vesper service," as a way of setting the tone for a serene end to the day. Like saying grace, a vesper service has religious overtones (It means "evening prayers"), but what I have in mind is uplifting music and a ritual of thinking about the day. Ask everyone:

- Who or what inspired you today? What kindness did you witness?
- What made you smile today?
- What's the best thing that happened today?

If your residential setting doesn't have such a group exercise at 5:00 p.m., try an individual ritual at bedtime. Teach aides or family members who assist residents in getting ready for bed to ask the person to name three specific things that brought him or her joy that day. Like a vesper service, it is a calming ritual to set the tone for a peaceful night's sleep. Families can easily adopt this practice, and it's good for *all* of us.

▶ Another variation:

Going to sleep happy is always a good thing, and I have long been an advocate for watching old Johnny Carson "Tonight" episodes to end the day with a smile on your face. Amazon offers the DVD collection, *The Ultimate Johnny Carson Collection—His Favorite Moments From The Tonight Show*, which works particularly well with older adults who may have seen many of these episodes when they first aired. But even if you are too young to have seen the original shows, the videos are likely to be amusing to people of all ages. You don't have to watch for long—10 or 15 minutes will do—so one DVD can provide many nights of pre-bedtime entertainment. But any short video that amuses you will do. My only caveat: Be prepared. If you're not going to watch Johnny Carson, pick out a video during the day when you are alert. Trying to find the

"just right" video when you are ready for sleep can be time-consuming and frustrating and could have an effect that is the opposite of what is intended.

▶ A variation for teachers:

Teachers can also create their own versions of closing rituals. An elementary school teacher can ask the questions above about inspiration, kindness, smile-makers and best things at the end of the day and perhaps lead the class in an uplifting song like, "I'd like to teach the world to sing (in perfect harmony)." Teachers who only see their students for an hour at a time, can still make a practice of ending their classes by complimenting the students for their attentiveness or hard work or positive attitude. Letting students know they are valued, that their teachers actually like spending time with them, can have tremendous positive impact over time.

And adding something fun to your classroom is another possibility. Maybe you start a class with a joke because relaxed learners learn more, and people anticipating a joke will arrive on time and settle down quickly. Or if you have some sort of viewing screen in your room, maybe you can end the class with a cartoon. This is also a great way to model appropriate humor.

Bottom line here: **Rituals are comforting, and can create positive habits.**

Chapter 4

"You don't have to say 'Hi' every time we pass each other!"

Cartoons provided by Glasbergen Cartoon Service

4) Welcome messages

In my file of random ideas gathered over decades is a simple sheet given to all guests at a Heritage Inn. The sheet does not provide a location, a copyright, or any information that I can offer for giving credit to that particular Heritage Inn, but it is a lovely example of how you might welcome guests to your hotel, your classroom, your residential care community, even your home. Here is my generic paraphrasing that you might adopt to suit your situation:

> Welcome.
>
> We hope you will find peace and rest while you are under our roof.
>
> May this be your second home. May those you love be

near you in thoughts and dreams, and may you be as comfortable and happy here as if you were in your own house.

May the business that brought you our way prosper, or if you are here on vacation, may you make happy memories. May every call you make and every message you receive, every person you meet and every new experience you have, add to your joy. When you leave, may you continue on safely.

We are all travelers on the journey of life. May these days be pleasant for you, profitable for society, helpful for those you meet, and a joy to those who know and love you best.

Blessings from your friends and the people who serve you at _____.

How might you adapt this for a classroom setting? Perhaps wishing the person inspiration, intellectual stimulation, opportunities for satisfying their curiosity, friendship…?

5) A delightful stroll

One of my favorite ideas is walking with a partner. Group walks are lovely, but carrying on a group conversation with half a dozen people or more is usually challenging, especially if some people in the group have hearing or mobility challenges. Two people walking can more easily have a conversation and set a pace that is comfortable for both of them. Encourage a friendly competition between them to find the most things to appreciate, such as singing birds, flowers blooming, sunshine, etc. The conversation will not only be positive, but the partners will truly enjoy the benefits of being outdoors. (Vital to everyone!)

Variations: This can obviously be practiced in senior settings and is great for spouses or friends who take regular walks. Whether or not they walk to and from school, also encourage students to take a "Find the beauty" stroll or "Find something funny or interesting." Creating a habit of paying attention to one's surroundings—mindfulness—has many benefits in other aspects of life, too. See also Chade-Meng Tan's book, *Joy on Demand*, which highlights the accumulated positive effect of noticing and appreciating life's small joys.

6) Discussion exercises

Activity leaders in senior settings are used to leading discussions, but often they center on current affairs in the news, which can be stressful. Here are a few ideas for generating happier thoughts that can be used by families, teachers and activity leaders:

- In the previous chapter, we suggested many possible themes for visual expressions of delight, such as comfort foods, conveniences and inventions, luxuries, and things that make you laugh. These could also be the basis for group discussions.

- One of the most intriguing questions to ask a group is, *"What if you woke up tomorrow with **only** what you were grateful for today?"* What would the members of the group have to be certain they included in today's gratitude list?

- Teach your group to practice micro-compassion. Make a list with your group of all the little things they can do for others, from simple courtesy (saying, *"Thank you"* and *"You're welcome"*), to making a crabby person smile, to inviting someone lonely to join you for an activity, to doing a chore without being asked, etc., etc. Once the list is made, get them to report each day what they did.

- Tell a story around a picture—either one that is funny or one that is poignant. Both can lead to discussions of the events, or people/animals shown and what we are grateful for as we discuss how the picture makes us feel or how it relates to something in our own lives. Google images under topics like "funny animals" or "poignant pictures," and you will have no shortage of visuals. Although it makes sense that moods are likely to be lifted by funny images, we are also uplifted by acts of kindness or pictures that arouse our empathy and help us feel connected to all of humanity. (This carrot picture comes from Shutterstock.com, but there are hundreds of pictures of foods—naturally formed or carved—that could inspire conversation. Sand sculptures and whimsical art are other fun topics to explore.)

- Also consider ordering our *Dinner Conversations* book for a wealth of topics and discussion questions that can be discussed with or without food.

7) Gratitude letter or visit

In 2011, John Kralik published a book titled, *A Simple Act of Gratitude: How Learning to Say Thank You Changed My Life*, in which he chronicled how he wrote 365 thank you notes—one a day for a year. Most of us don't have the discipline to do the same, but we can do *something*. Lead a letter-writing group in which residents or students write a note to someone who has influenced their lives in a positive way. Also encourage family members to write such letters to one another.

- It's important to note that the simple act of *thinking* of someone with gratitude will lift the writer's spirit. For example, if I write a letter to the teacher who instilled in me a love of art history, I will feel good thinking about that person's influence even if I have no idea where she is today or even if she's still alive, and therefore can't send it.

- Sent letters have the added benefit of not only the lift from the act of writing, but the imagined pleasure of the person receiving the letter. And sometimes you will get a reply, which is even more affirming.

- As with compliments, encourage the writers to be specific—not just, *"Thanks for being a good teacher,"* but what the person did and how it influenced the writer. Still, letters don't need to be long or serious.

- Some people are doubtful of their writing abilities, and would rather send a carefully-chosen greeting card. That's fine, but even then, show that it was carefully chosen by adding a note at the bottom, such as: *This card expresses exactly what I want you to know.*

- Research has shown that a gratitude *visit*—thanking a person face to face—has greater influence on the visitor's wellbeing than simply writing a letter. In a residential care setting where the intended recipient lives elsewhere, this may not be possible. Nor can students too young to drive necessarily make such a visit. Nevertheless, you can create a habit of face-to-face thank you's within your residence, home, or school that will create an inviting atmosphere.

- Hand-written notes or cards are wonderful because they show the effort of the writer and are tangible reminders that a person can look at again and again, but technology has given us other ways to reach out to one another. Leaving a *voice mail message* is one. I have a friend who daily plays a saved message from a beloved grandson who recorded how he loved and missed her and wanted to come visit. See also the *email idea* from Allen Klein below.

- Do you have a sunshine committee to send cheerful greetings to someone who is ill or enduring a crisis? If not, form one.

- And consider more reasons than gratitude for making contact. Have you ever gone about your daily business, and suddenly a happy memory of something funny that happened between an old friend and you pops into your head? If the friend is reachable, let him know. Or if you share a common sense of humor, send a cartoon or joke or share a YouTube video link.

Chapter 4

"I try to live each day as if it were my last."

Cartoons provided by Glasbergen Cartoon Service

An idea from Allen Klein:

Allen Klein is the author of *The Healing Power of Humor*, *The Courage to Laugh*, and literally dozens of other books (See Resources). In 2016, he decided to send an email to one person a day for every day of the year. He attached the graphic you see here, and simply said, "I appreciate you being in my life. You have enriched my life in some way." As you can see, he didn't say *how* the recipient enriched his life, which generally goes against what we have said about being specific. Instead, he put his energy into thinking about *who* he would thank each day without planning ahead. That act of reviewing the far flung influencers in his life was his daily reward—a counting of his blessings. But as you might expect, many of the recipients were surprised to be on his radar and wrote back thanking him for his encouragement and noting that it came just when they needed it—how did he know? Those thanks (and sometimes renewed contact) added to his sense of reward for a good deed. The experience has been so positive that he encourages others to adopt it.

8) Gratitude/humor/happiness journal

Keeping a gratitude journal is probably the most common suggestion for a self-imposed gratitude ritual, and has the advantage of being enduring—something you can have pleasure in re-reading. Consider making a journal a possible short-term focus for a writing group you lead, but keep in mind:

- Like compliments, entries must be specific. Writing every day that you are grateful for *"family and friends"* does nothing for your wellbeing. *Terrific phone call with my daughter today about her career change* doesn't say a lot, but says enough.

- Like a gratitude tree, this ritual can get old fast. You might keep it up for two or three weeks; then try something else for a month or two before coming back to it for a while. It takes time and discipline to create a ritual habit, but once created, if it becomes an onerous obligation instead of a joy, it's time to try something new.

Like everything else we have mentioned, lighthearted events are likely to make for the happiest memories. Therefore, a variation of this is to keep a **Smile Journal** and record in it anything that happens that makes you smile—or laugh out loud—on any given day. If you can't think of anything that amused you on a particular day, go back in your memory bank and write about past things that still make you smile. Again, these should be specific, but don't need to be long. "Poncho video" is enough to release a pile of happy endorphins in me because it is both a broad memory of a terrific trip to New Zealand with my daughters and a specific memory of our mutual laughter on a windy, rainy day as they recorded me trying to get my head through a bright yellow poncho that enveloped my body, but seemed to be devoid of the proper openings. (You can view it on our website at www.CreatingDelight.com).

9) Journaling cards

Bron introduced me to journaling cards. The ones we used for the black and white "tree" on page 44 are from Project Life

(http://beckyhiggins.com/project-life/), and although they seem to have been intended for people who want to organize their lives in scrapbooks, precisely because they come in many designs and color schemes, they are well-suited to be put to other uses. (Drop this sentence: We used mostly black and white cards for one of our "gratitude trees" by punching a hole in one corner and adding a subtle ribbon.)

Bron has long used the cards in a variety of her workshops. When you are encouraging someone to write down something she is grateful for or something amusing, having a cheery card to write on seems to foster inspiration. The Project Life cards come in two sizes, 2 inches by 4 inches (roughly 5 x 10 cm) and 3 by 4 inches. The smaller version has 96 cards and 12 designs to a pack. One of the reasons Bron likes journaling cards over journals is that you can put them in a box and access them randomly; after you've accumulated a dozen or more, whenever you need to cheer yourself up, pull one out and surprise yourself!

See also the card samples on pages 60 and 61 for more possibilities.

You can, of course, make your own cards. Circles or rectangles will do, or any of the other designs we used for the "gratitude trees" might also be put in a box. My dentist has fish-shaped notecards at the checkout desk, which patients are encouraged to write on at the end of their visit and put in a clear glass bowl marked "Fishing for feedback."

The creative act of a decorating a card is its own pleasure, (Think play!) and can help inspire what you write on it, Likewise, boxes to keep them in are fun to decorate. The possibilities are limitless.

Another variation is to **make these cards into a gift**. For a milestone birthday, a friend received a decorated box, and in it were circles that had been distributed to family and friends by (and then returned to) her daughter. On each circle was written a "Why I love you" message. You can be sure that friend will always treasure it and can turn to it on a down day. You could create other versions, such as:

- Why I admire you

- Why you make me smile/laugh

- What I hope for you

And birthdays are not the only occasions that would be appropriate. Think of it as an end-of-the-year school project, for example, that students could do for one another—each student writing one card for every other student in the class. Or as an encouragement gesture for someone going through a tough time. Or to celebrate a holiday.

10) Create Good Fortunes

Chinese restaurants send us on our way with fortunes folded into hard cookies. For years, Donald Lau, a vice-president with Wonton Foods, wrote many of the fortunes for his company's cookies, using any resource he could find for inspiration. One of his last fortunes—before he ran out of ideas entirely—was taken from a subway sign:

"Beware of odors from unfamiliar sources."

Meg Barnhouse, author of *Did I Say That Out Loud? Musings from a Questioning Soul*, (See Resources), may have gotten one

of Mr. Lau's last efforts when she opened a cookie with the "utterly lame" proverb, "Where there's a will, there's a way." If she owned a fortune cookie company, she said, she would write fortunes that "excited the imagination, shone a light on new possibilities, and shifted perspectives."

For example, she might write, "You will see three beautiful things tomorrow." The person receiving that fortune would look for beauty all through the next day, perhaps in places he never looked before. Perhaps he would find *more* than three things beautiful and then would begin to contemplate which were the *most* beautiful things he saw. Wouldn't *that* balance out the horrors of the evening news?

Or she might write: "Seven people love you madly." Think of the fun of imagining who those people might be! Could it be someone you least expect?

Or she might give someone's worries a little respite: "You will figure something out two days from now."

Or she might give someone permission to take an intermission: "Don't try to improve yourself tomorrow," or "The next two years are just for fun."

Putting that idea into action, now when guests come to dinner at her home, she offers them (literally) a good fortune in a bowl (minus the cookie) as a happy parting gift. You can do the same. Register on our website (www.CreatingDelight.com) to access a template for this exercise that includes details, and sample possible "good fortunes" that include both uplifting and funny quotes.

Chapter 4

11) Think fun

Messages —in whatever form they take—don't have to be serious. Consider thanking someone for:

- Sharing a funny video, cartoon, joke, greeting card
- Making you laugh at lunch
- Teaching you something fun to do with your kids
- Sharing cute pictures of a pet or grandchild
- Smiling no matter what happens

"You're getting pretty good at this stress management thing."

Cartoons provided by Glasbergen Cartoon Service

Resources

Books

In creating a resource list, we started out trying to separate the books into categories, but it was soon obvious that many authors fit into multiple categories. Furthermore, we realized that just because a book was aimed at educators did not mean people dealing with an aging population might not benefit from the author's ideas.

Ultimately, we have combined them all, letting you make your own decisions. If you are reading this list on Kindle or on our website, the books are linked to Amazon; click on any title and you can read much more about it with no obligation to purchase. Also note that many of the authors have written multiple books; you can also peruse those via Amazon, and click on the back arrow to come back to the highlighted book or the website. You can, of course, look for books on Amazon by a category, but be prepared to find gazillions. Amazon lists more than 105,000 books on happiness and many thousands more on gratitude, humor, and play, which means we could have (perhaps should have) included many more titles, but we didn't want to overwhelm you completely!

One way we tried to put some limits on this list was to focus on books that were less than 10 years old, but we made exceptions for classics and books we didn't want you to miss. We welcome your suggestions for additions and your critique of what we have included.

- Achor, Shawn. *The Happiness Advantage: The Seven Principles of Positive Psychology That Fuel Success and Performance at Work* (2010)

- Barnhouse, Meg. *Did I Say That Out Loud? Musings from a Questioning Soul* (2006)

- Bateson, Patrick. *Play, Playfulness, Creativity, and Innovation*, (2013)

- Berk, Ronald. *Humor as an Instructional Defibrillator: Evidence-Based Techniques in Teaching and Assessment* (2002)

- Berk, Ronald A. and Buxman, Karyn. *Top Secret Tips for Successful Humor in the Workplace* (2009)

- Brown, Brene. *The Gifts of Imperfection: Let Go of Who You Think You're Supposed to Be and Embrace Who You Are* (2010)

- Brown, Stuart. *Play: How it Shapes the Brain, Opens the Imagination, and Invigorates the Soul*, (2009)

- Buettner, Dan. *Thrive: Finding Happiness the Blue Zones Way* (2011)

- Buxman, Karyn. *Amazed and Amused: How to Survive and Thrive as a Healthcare Professional* (2012)

- Burkeman, Oliver. *The Antidote: Happiness for People Who Can't Stand Positive Thinking* (2012)

- Clinton, Max. *How to be Witty (For Someone Who is Not): The definitive manual to being funny, clever, witty, and owning it in social environments* (2015)

- Cohen, Gene D. MD, PhD. *The Mature Mind: The Positive Power of the Aging Brain* (2006)

- Cousins, Norman. *Head First: The Biology of Hope and the Healing Power of the Human Spirit* (1990)

- Csikszentmihalyi, Mihaly. *Flow: The Psychology of Optimal Experience* (1990) and *Creativity: The Psychology of Discovery and Invention,* (2013).

- The Dalai Lama and Desmond Tutu, with authorship assistance from Douglas Abrams. *The Book of Joy: Lasting Happiness in a Changing World* (2016)

- De Koven, Bernard. *A Playful Path,* (2014), and *The Well-Played Game,* (2013).

- Dweck, Carol. *Mindset: The New Psychology of Success* (2007)

- Elkind, David. *The Power of Play: Learning What Comes Naturally*, (2007)

- Elsagher, Brenda. *Your Glasses Are on Top of Your Head,* (2015)

- Emmons, Robert A. *Gratitude Works!: A 21-Day Program for Creating Emotional Prosperity* (2013) and *Thanks!: How Practicing Gratitude Can Make You Happier.* (2008)

- Epperson, Kelly. *365 Days of Joy* (2010)

- Franzini, Louis R. *Kids Who Laugh: How to Develop Your Child's Sense of Humor* (2002) and *Just Kidding: Using Humor Effectively* (2015)

- Geisel, Theodore (Dr. Seuss). *You're Only Old Once* (1986)

- Gerberg, Mort (editor). *Last Laughs, Cartoons about Aging, Retirement . . . and the Beyond* (2007)

- Gesell, Izzy. *Playing Along, (37 Group Learning Activities)* (1997).

- Gianoulis, Nick and Measley, Nat. *Playing it Forward: Because Fun Matters for Employees, Customers and Bottom Line* (2015)

- Gilbert, Daniel. *Stumbling on Happiness* (2007)

- Gray, Peter. *Free to Learn: Why Unleashing the Instinct to Play Will Make Our Children Happier, More Self-Reliant, and Better Students for Life* (2015)

- Hanson, Rick. *Hardwiring Happiness: The New Brain Science of Contentment, Calm, and Confidence* (2013)

- Hemsath, Dave & Yerkes, Leslie, *301 Ways to Have Fun at Work,* (1997)

- Henslin, Earl. *This is Your Brain on Joy A Revolutionary Program for Balancing Mood, Restoring Brain Health, and Nurturing Spiritual Growth* (2011)

- Hoare, Joe. *Awakening the Laughter Buddha Within* and *Everyday Stress Busters*

- Jasheway, Leigh Anne. *101 Comedy Games for Children and Grown-Ups* (2014)

- Kaufman, Scott & Gregoire, Carolyn. *Wired to Create: Unraveling the Mysteries of the Creative Mind* (2015)

- Kaufman, Scott & Paul, Elliot. *The Philosophy of Creativity: New Essays* (2014)

- Kaufman, Scott. *Ungifted: Intelligence Redefined* (2015)

- Klein, Allen. He's literally written dozens. These are his classics and a few of his most recent titles: *The Healing Power of Humor,* (1989) *The Courage to Laugh,* (1998) *You Can't Ruin My Day,* (2015), and *Always Look on the Bright Side,* (2013)

Resources

- Kralik, John. *A Simple Act of Gratitude: How Learning to Say Thank You Changed My Life.* (2011)

- Langer, Ellen. *The Power of Mindful Learning* (1998)

- Lundberg, Elaine & Thurston, Cheryl. *If They're Laughing, They Just Might be Listening: Ideas for Using Humor Effectively in the Classroom—Even if You're Not Funny Yourself* (2002)

- Lyubomirsky, Sonja. *The How of Happiness: A New Approach to Getting the Life You Want* (2008)

- Madson, Patricia Ryan. *Improv Wisdom: Don't Prepare, Just Show Up* (2006)

- McGhee, Paul, PhD. *Humor As Survival Training for a Stressed-Out World: The 7 Humor Habits Program* (2010)

- Mellin, Laurel. *Wired for Joy* (2010)

- Miller, Dr. Michael. *Heal Your Heart: The Positive Emotions Prescription to Prevent and Reverse Heart Disease* (2014)

- Moon, Susan. *This Is Getting Old: Zen Thoughts on Aging with Humor and Dignity* (2010)

- Morrison, Mary Kay. *Using Humor to Maximize Living* (2013) and *Using Humor to Maximize Learning* (2010)

- Paulson, Terry. *The Optimism Advantage: 50 Simple Truths to Transform Your Attitudes and Actions into Results*

- Pellis, Sergio & Pellis, Vivien. *The Playful Brain; Venturing to the Limits of Neuroscience* (2010)

- Petras, Kathryn and Ross. *Age doesn't matter unless you're a cheese* (2002)

- Robinson, Ken. *Out of Our Minds: Learning to be Creative*, (2013)

- Robinson, Vera. *Humor and the Health Professions* (1990)

- Roggenbuck, Adrianne. *Score 3: Super Closers, Openers, Revisiters, Energizers*

- Rosenblatt, Roger. *Rules for Aging* (2000)

- Rubin, Gretchen. *The Happiness Project: Or, Why I Spent a Year Trying to Sing in the Morning, Clean My Closets, Fight Right, Read Aristotle, and Generally Have More Fun* (2011)

- Sacks, Oliver. *Gratitude* (2015)

- Schwartz, Joel L, MD. *Noses Are Red—How to Nurture Your Child's Sense of Humor* (2006)

- Seligman, Martin. *Authentic Happiness: Using the New Positive Psychology to Realize Your Potential for Lasting Fulfillment* (2002) and *Flourish: A Visionary New Understanding of Happiness and Well-being* (2012)

- Sherbert, Susan. *Grown-ups Don't Skip: Have FUN Be Happy Enjoy Life* (2013)

- Sicart, Miguel. *Play Matters*, (2014)

- Stephenson, Sue. *Kidding Around: Connecting Kids to Happiness, Laughter and Humor* (2015)

- Tamblyn, Doni. *Laugh and Learn: 95 Ways to Use Humor for More Effective Teaching and Training* (2006)

Resources

- Tamblyn, Doni & Weiss, Sharon. *The Big Book of Humorous Training Games* (2000)

- Tan, Chade-Meng. *Joy on Demand* (2016)

- Tarvin, Andrew. *Humor That Works: 501 Ways to Use Humor to Beat Stress, Increase Productivity and Have Fun at Work* (2012)

- Thich Nhat Hanh. *Happiness: Essential Mindfulness Practices* (2005)

- Ulbrich, Carla. *How Can You NOT Laugh at a Time Like This?: Reclaim Your Health with Humor, Creativity, and Grit* (2011)

- von Oech, Roger. *A Whack on the Side of the Head,* (2008)

- von Oech, Roger. *A Kick in the Seat of the Pants,* (1986)

- Weems, Scott. *Ha! The Science of When We Laugh and Why* (2014)

- Weinstein, Matt & Goodman, Joel. *Playfair,* (1983)

- Wooten, Patty. *Heart, Humor and Healing* (1994)

Not included in this list are craft books that provide ideas for decorating cards, messages, and boxes related to visual delight projects. We expect to highlight some in the future or put demonstrations on our website (www.CreatingDelight.com), but for the purposes of this book, the choices were simply too broad. Even attempting to choose a book to teach Zentangles (the technique used on our sample footprint) was too daunting, although you may get many craft book ideas from the suppliers' websites listed below.

Resources for our visual versions supplies

As noted earlier, we feel strongly that whatever form your "gratitude tree" takes, it should be visually appealing, adding eye-catching color and beauty to the room or the outdoor space it occupies. We also believe in finding bargains wherever possible, and after exhausting our own supply closets, found lots of useful materials in dollar stores (U.S.) and $2 shops (Australia), charity shops, and flea markets as well as in more traditional craft, art, party, and office supply stores.

You can also get ideas and find supplies by visiting these stores' websites. Here are some potential online sources:

- https://www.createforless.com/
- http://www6.discountschoolsupply.com/
- https://www.etsy.com/
- http://www.hobbycraft.co.uk/
- http://www.joann.com/
- https://www.lincraft.com.au/
- http://www.michaels.com/
- http://riotstores.com.au/
- https://store.schoolspecialty.com/
- https://www.spotlightstores.com/
- http://www.stockade.ca/Craft-Supplies
- http://www.theworks.co.uk/c/craft-supplies

Thank you to Randy Glasbergen

The cartoons in this manuscript were created by Randy Glasbergen who died unexpectedly in 2015, and whose family is keeping his legacy alive "until the world no longer needs to laugh"—definitely a long-term obligation. I have always enjoyed Mr. Glasbergen's ability to find literally thousands of captions for simple scenarios. He has dozens of captions for two fish in a fish bowl, and many more for penguins, snails, centipedes, hens, dogs, cats, and other creatures—plus humans, of course. I urge you to check out the possibilities for adding laughter to your day at www.Glasbergen.com.

Miscellaneous comments

Bedtime entertainment: If you want to take us up on the idea of going to sleep after watching something funny, *The Ultimate Johnny Carson Collection—His Favorite Moments From The Tonight Show* is available on Amazon, along with dozens of other DVDs from his show. But you will also find many other choices to tickle your funny bone that are free on YouTube. Surprisingly, it's harder to find anything from Jay Leno's years of hosting the *Tonight Show* after Johnny Carson, but you will find lots of videos on *Jay Leno's Garage*, which may be pleasing to some. There are a few excerpts of the *David Letterman Show* and many of the British *Graham Norton Show*. Comedy, we hope, has no national borders.

We have suggested late night talk shows because it is easy to watch parts of them—perhaps a 10 minute excerpt—without having to watch a whole episode of a sitcom, for example, that simply keeps you awake longer. Sleepy Time tea and a little laughter is a shortcut to relaxation.

Boxes for journaling cards: As we noted, we love the many designs for journaling cards that we found from Project Life, and Etsy (https://www.etsy.com/market/journaling_cards) has many more. But we also spent a lot of time looking for a box that neatly fit the 2x4 inch (5x10 cm) and 3x4 inch card sizes. The only one that seemed to be a perfect fit was a tin box sold at stores offering gift cards. It is meant as a decorative way to hold that gift card, but it doesn't hold a lot of journaling cards. Nevertheless, the red and white one with "Joy" on the lid that we found for December holiday shoppers was highly appealing.

The alternatives to scouring stores for a perfect-fit box is to a) find a box you like and make your own cards to fit them or b) find a "bigger than needed or big-enough" box—tin, cardboard, papier-mâché, or wood—and decorate it any way you please. We think the latter has lots of possibilities for another fun project of its own.

Making your own decorative journaling cards or decorative cards for hanging on some variation of a visual delight "tree," is also a terrific group project.

Other things we offer:

◆ If you are interested in learning more about how to bring our ideas to your setting, contact us about a webinar or workshop.

◆ Our website, www.CreatingDelight.com, offers many downloadable exercises and ideas free to those who register, and as noted above, we will be adding more over time.

◆ We welcome your ideas and input relating your successes, cautions, and resources. You can contact us at info@CreatingDelight.com, or visit our Facebook group page at https://www.facebook.com/creatingdelight/.

The future

We see the umbrella of Creating Delight as huge. If in this book it connects gratitude, humor, and play, in future iterations watch for creativity, improvisational theatre, laughter practices, brain fun, and more. We hope the conversation has just begun.

Who we are

Kathy Laurenhue, CEO (Chief Enthusiasm Officer) of Wiser Now, Inc. (www.WiserNow.com) has put her master's degree in Instructional Technology (training) to work in the field of aging for 30+ years throughout the U.S. and Australia. Although she built her reputation on her work in dementia care, for the last dozen+ years her focus has been on the broader field of wellbeing in aging and providing positive stimulation for the minds of *all* older adults as well as intergenerational audiences. She is the author of four books, dozens of downloadable courses, plus literally thousands of word games, trivia quizzes, discussion topics, and creative training exercises. She is known for providing practical information that can be instantly put to use and delivering it in a lighthearted manner.

Bron Roberts is CFO (Chief Happiness Officer) of Let's Laugh (www.letslaugh.com.au). With over 35 years' experience as a meditation and stress management trainer, almost as long as a humor and laughter consultant, and a humor-filled presentation style that is guaranteed to get groups laughing, Bron keeps participants engaged from the first moment till the last. She is a fully certified Laughter Yoga Leader Trainer and trained as a 'Laughter Boss' under the guidance of Dr. Peter Spitzer through the Clown Doctors and Humour Foundation. Bron's passion for creating healthier, happier individuals, communities and workplaces not only makes her a popular media interview subject, but ensures that Let's Laugh presentations set the stage for lasting change in individuals and organizations. For proof, check out the list of 150+ clients and the broad sampling of testimonials on her website.

Sharon Wall (www.ageingbycaring.com.au) is a nurse with a Masters of Public Health and over 35 years working in the aged care sector. As the director of "Ageing by Caring Pty Ltd," she enhances the experience of ageing by caring, communicating, and creating. She provides education and training, strategic planning, policy development and management, review and evaluation + leadership development focused on mentorship and coaching. She's published widely in the areas of dementia, Aboriginal Ageing, Multicultural Ageing, and Advance Care Planning. Sharon has a long standing association with the Clown Doctors and Humour Foundation through a valued association with the wonderful and much loved Peter Spitzer (1946-2014). Peter (aka Dr Fruit-Loop, Spitzer's clown doctor alter ego) was the founder of the Australian Clown Doctor Program. She currently acknowledges Peter's lasting legacy as she prepares Elder Clowns to work in aged care settings by providing them with dementia training and support.

Kathy and Bron met each other through their longtime membership in the Association for Applied and Therapeutic Humor (www.AATH.org), and are both Certified Humor Professionals. Kathy and Sharon first met through their collaboration on an Australian aged care project more than a dozen years ago.

Workshops and Webinars

All three of us offer workshops and webinars on a variety of topics. Kathy and Bron are the presenters for **Creating Delight by Connecting Gratitude, Humor, and Play**. Here's some basic information:

We see a clear difference between environment and atmosphere. When someone walks into your classroom, residential care community, or home, the environment may not say "Wow!" and getting to wow may require a big budget. But a beautiful physical environment doesn't guarantee a welcoming atmosphere, and fortunately, creating an *atmospheric* wow requires only an abundant *attitude* budget.

Summary:

In this inter-active 3.5 hour workshop, we will:

- Provide research-based evidence of the positive physical and mental effects of gratitude, humor and play and illustrate how they are intertwined;

- Teach participants how to give and receive compliments to set the stage for expressing gratitude and creating an inviting atmosphere;

- Give examples of at least 10 ways to incorporate gratitude, humor, and play rituals into daily life; and

- Give participants hands-on experience in making three variations of a gratitude "tree."

Participants will return to their communities with easy and practical ways to change and recharge the atmosphere in their environments and with it, the lives of those they serve.